More Advance Praise for *Deaf Republic*

"Pulse-quickening, glinting like unburied ore, grounded equally in the imaginative, political, moral, and personal realms, *Deaf Republic* is a thunderclap book. American poetry needs what Ilya Kaminsky's performative, possibility-enlarging, boundlessly surprising pages bring to it. Or at least, I do."
—Jane Hirshfield

"*Deaf Republic* is a stunning and prescient drama, like the best books of Márquez and Kundera. Not many American poets, not many poets anywhere, are engaged in this kind of work. I think that *Deaf Republic* will be a splendid, groundbreaking moment. Reading this book, my overwhelming sense is admiration and pleasure."
—Kwame Dawes

"*Deaf Republic* is a perfectly extraordinary book. It is so romantic, and so painful, with such a stunning lightness of touch but such devastating weight. It speaks forward and backward, directly to—and beautifully beyond—the time of its creation in the way that only truly great literature does. I will keep reading it, again and again, as the world turns. I feel quite sure my grandchildren will read this book. It's one of those."
—Max Porter

Praise for Ilya Kaminsky

"Kaminsky is more than a promising young poet; he is a poet of promise fulfilled. I am in awe of his gifts."
—Carolyn Forché

"Ilya Kaminsky proceeds like a perfect gardener—he grafts the gifts of the Russian newer literary tradition on the American tree of poetry and forgetting."
—Adam Zagajewski

"Passionate, daring to laugh and weep, direct and unexpected, Ilya Kaminsky's poetry has a glorious tilt and scope."
—Robert Pinsky

"With his magical style in English, [Kaminsky's] poems . . . seem like a literary counterpart to Chagall in which laws of gravity have been suspended and colors reassigned, but only to make everyday reality that much more indelible. His imagination is so transformative that we respond with equal measures of grief and exhilaration."
—American Academy of Arts and Letters citation
for the Addison M. Metcalf Award

DEAF REPUBLIC

Also by Ilya Kaminsky

POETRY

Dancing in Odessa (2004)
Musica Humana (chapbook, 2003)

TRANSLATIONS

Dark Elderberry Branch: Poems of Marina Tsvetaeva (2012) with Jean Valentine
Mourning Ploughs the Winter: Poems of Guy Jean (2012) with Katie Farris
This Lamentable City: Poems of Polina Barskova (2010) with Katie Farris,
   Rachel Galvin, and Matthew Zapruder

ANTHOLOGIES

In the Shape of a Human Body I Am Visiting the Earth: Poems from Far and Wide (2017)
   with Dominic Luxford and Jesse Nathan
Gossip and Metaphysics: Russian Modernist Poems and Prose (2014) with Katie Farris
   and Valzhyna Mort
A God in the House: Poets Talk about Faith (2012) with Katherine Towler
Homage to Paul Celan (2012) with G. C. Waldrep
The Ecco Anthology of International Poetry (2010) with Susan Harris

DEAF REPUBLIC

Poems

Ilya Kaminsky

Graywolf Press

This publication is made possible, in part, by the voters of Minnesota through a Minnesota State Arts Board Operating Support grant, thanks to a legislative appropriation from the arts and cultural heritage fund, and a grant from the Wells Fargo Foundation. Significant support has also been provided by the National Endowment for the Arts, Target, the McKnight Foundation, the Lannan Foundation, the Amazon Literary Partnership, and other generous contributions from foundations, corporations, and individuals. To these organizations and individuals we offer our heartfelt thanks.

Published by Graywolf Press
250 Third Avenue North, Suite 600
Minneapolis, Minnesota 55401

www.graywolfpress.org

Published in the United States of America

ISBN 978-1-55597-831-0

   4 6 8 10 9 7 5 3

Library of Congress Control Number: 2018947088

Cover design: Kapo Ng

Cover art: Gail Schneider

Interior illustrations: Jennifer Whitten

Contents

We Lived Happily during the War / 3

Deaf Republic / 5

Dramatis Personae / 7

ACT ONE: THE TOWNSPEOPLE TELL THE STORY OF SONYA AND ALFONSO

Gunshot / 11

As Soldiers March, Alfonso Covers the Boy's Face with a Newspaper / 12

Alfonso, in Snow / 13

Deafness, an Insurgency, Begins / 14

Alfonso Stands Answerable / 15

That Map of Bone and Opened Valves / 16

The Townspeople Circle the Boy's Body / 17

Of Weddings before the War / 18

Still Newlyweds / 19

Soldiers Aim at Us / 20

Checkpoints / 22

Before the War, We Made a Child / 23

As Soldiers Choke the Stairwell / 24

4 a.m. Bombardment / 25

Arrival / 26

Lullaby / 27

Question / 28

While the Child Sleeps, Sonya Undresses / 29

A Cigarette / 30

A Dog Sniffs / 31

What We Cannot Hear / 32

Central Square / 33

A Widower / 34

For His Wife / 35

I, This Body / 36

Her Dresses / 37

Elegy / 38

Above Blue Tin Roofs, Deafness / 39

A City Like a Guillotine Shivers on Its Way to the Neck / 40

In the Bright Sleeve of the Sky / 41

To Live / 42

The Townspeople Watch Them Take Alfonso / 43

Away / 44

Eulogy / 45

Question / 46

Such Is the Story Made of Stubbornness and a Little Air / 47

ACT TWO: THE TOWNSPEOPLE TELL THE STORY OF MOMMA GALYA

Townspeople Speak of Galya on Her Green Bicycle / 51

When Momma Galya First Protested / 52

A Bundle of Laundry / 53

What Are Days / 54

Galya Whispers, as Anushka Nuzzles / 55

Galya's Puppeteers / 56

In Bombardment, Galya / 57

The Little Bundles / 58

Galya's Toast / 59

Theater Nights / 60

And While Puppeteers Are Arrested / 61

Soldiers Don't Like Looking Foolish / 62

Search Patrols / 63

Lullaby / 64

Firing Squad / 65

Question / 66

Yet, I Am / 67

The Trial / 68

Pursued by the Men of Vasenka / 69

Anonymous / 70

And Yet, on Some Nights / 71

In a Time of Peace / 75

DEAF REPUBLIC

We Lived Happily during the War

And when they bombed other people's houses, we

protested
but not enough, we opposed them but not

enough. I was
in my bed, around my bed America

was falling: invisible house by invisible house by invisible house—

I took a chair outside and watched the sun.

In the sixth month
of a disastrous reign in the house of money

in the street of money in the city of money in the country of money,
our great country of money, we (forgive us)

lived happily during the war.

Deaf Republic

Dramatis Personae

TOWNSPEOPLE OF VASENKA—the chorus, "we" who tell the story, and on balconies, the wind fondles laundry lines.

ALFONSO BARABINSKI—puppeteer, Sonya's newlywed husband, and the "I" of Act One.

SONYA BARABINSKI—Vasenka's best puppeteer, Alfonso's newlywed wife, and pregnant.

CHILD—inside Sonya, seahorse-sized, sleeping, and later, Anushka.

PETYA—deaf boy, Sonya's cousin.

MOMMA GALYA ARMOLINSKAYA—puppet theater owner, instigates insurgency, and the "I" of Act Two.

GALYA'S PUPPETEERS—teach signs from the theater balcony, as if regulating traffic:
    for *Soldier*—finger like a beak pecks one eye.
    for *Snitch*—fingers peck both eyes.
    for *Army Jeep*—clenched fist moves forward.

SOLDIERS—arrive in Vasenka to "protect our freedom," speaking a language no one understands.

PUPPETS—hang on doors and porches of the families of the arrested, except for one puppet lying on the cement: a middle-aged woman wearing a child like a broken arm, her mouth filling with snow.

ACT ONE

The Townspeople Tell the Story of Sonya and Alfonso

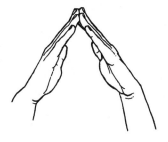

Town

Gunshot

Our country is the stage.

When soldiers march into town, public assemblies are officially prohibited. But today, neighbors flock to the piano music from Sonya and Alfonso's puppet show in Central Square. Some of us have climbed up into trees, others hide behind benches and telegraph poles.

When Petya, the deaf boy in the front row, sneezes, the sergeant puppet collapses, shrieking. He stands up again, snorts, shakes his fist at the laughing audience.

An army jeep swerves into the square, disgorging its own Sergeant.

Disperse immediately!

Disperse immediately! the puppet mimics in a wooden falsetto.

Everyone freezes except Petya, who keeps giggling. Someone claps a hand over his mouth. The Sergeant turns toward the boy, raising his finger.

You!

You! the puppet raises a finger.

Sonya watches her puppet, the puppet watches the Sergeant, the Sergeant watches Sonya and Alfonso, but the rest of us watch Petya lean back, gather all the spit in his throat, and launch it at the Sergeant.

The sound we do not hear lifts the gulls off the water.

As Soldiers March, Alfonso Covers the Boy's Face with a Newspaper

Fourteen people, most of us strangers,
watch Sonya kneel by Petya

shot in the middle of the street.
She picks up his spectacles shining like two coins, balances them on his nose.

Observe this moment
—how it convulses—

Snow falls and the dogs run into the streets like medics.

Fourteen of us watch:
Sonya kisses his forehead—her shout a hole

torn in the sky, it shimmers the park benches, porchlights.
We see in Sonya's open mouth

the nakedness
of a whole nation.

She stretches out
beside the little snowman napping in the middle of the street.

As picking up its belly the country runs.

Alfonso, in Snow

You are alive, I whisper to myself, *therefore something in you listens.*

Something runs down the street, falls, fails to get up.
I run etcetera with my legs and my hands behind
my pregnant wife etcetera down Vasenka Street I run it
only takes a few minutes etcetera to make a man.

Deafness, an Insurgency, Begins

Our country woke up next morning and refused to hear soldiers.

In the name of Petya, we refuse.

At six a.m., when soldiers compliment girls in the alleyway, the girls slide by, pointing to their ears. At eight, the bakery door is shut in soldier Ivanoff's face, though he's their best customer. At ten, Momma Galya chalks NO ONE HEARS YOU on the gates of the soldiers' barracks.

By eleven a.m., arrests begin.

Our hearing doesn't weaken, but something silent in us strengthens.

After curfew, families of the arrested hang homemade puppets out of their windows. The streets empty but for the squeaks of strings and the *tap tap*, against the buildings, of wooden fists and feet.

In the ears of the town, snow falls.

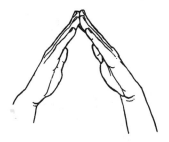

Town

Alfonso Stands Answerable

My people, you were really something fucking fine
on the morning of first arrests:

our men, once frightened, bound to their beds, now stand up like human masts—
deafness passes through us like a police whistle.

Here then I
testify:

each of us
comes home, shouts at a wall, at a stove, at a refrigerator, at himself. Forgive me, I

was not honest with you,
life—

to you I stand answerable.
I run etcetera with my legs and my hands etcetera I run down Vasenka Street etcetera—

Whoever listens:
thank you for the feather on my tongue,

thank you for our argument that ends, thank you for deafness,
Lord, such fire

from a match you never lit.

That Map of Bone and Opened Valves

I watched the Sergeant aim, the deaf boy take iron and fire in his mouth—
his face on the asphalt,
that map of bone and opened valves.
It's the air. Something in the air wants us too much.
The earth is still.
The tower guards eat cucumber sandwiches.
This first day
soldiers examine the ears of bartenders, accountants, soldiers—
the wicked things silence does to soldiers.
They tear Gora's wife from her bed like a door off a bus.
Observe this moment
—how it convulses—
The body of the boy lies on the asphalt like a paperclip.
The body of the boy lies on the asphalt
like the body of a boy.
I touch the walls, feel the pulse of the house, and I
stare up wordless and do not know why I am alive.
We tiptoe this city,
Sonya and I,
between theaters and gardens and wrought-iron gates—
Be courageous, we say, but no one
is courageous, as a sound we do not hear
lifts the birds off the water.

The Townspeople Circle the Boy's Body

The dead boy's body still lies in the square.

Sonya spoons him on the cement. Inside her—her child sleeps. Momma Galya brings Sonya a pillow. A man in a wheelchair brings a gallon of milk.

Alfonso lies next to them in the snow. Wraps one arm around her belly. He puts one hand to the ground. He hears the cars stop, doors slam, dogs bark. When he pulls his hand off the ground, he hears nothing.

Behind them, a puppet lies on cement, mouth filling with snow.

Forty minutes later, it is morning. Soldiers step back into the square.

The townspeople lock arms to form a circle and another circle around that circle and another circle to keep the soldiers from the boy's body.

We watch Sonya stand (the child inside her straightens its leg). Someone has given her a sign, which she holds high above her head: THE PEOPLE ARE DEAF.

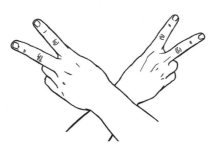

The town watches

Of Weddings before the War

Yes, I bought you a wedding dress big enough for the two of us
and in the taxi home
we kissed a coin from your mouth to mine.

The landlady might've noticed
a drizzle of stains on the sheets—
angels could do it more neatly

but they don't. I can still climb your
underwear, *my ass
is smaller than yours!*

You pat my cheek,
beam—
may you win the lottery and spend it all on doctors!

You are two fingers more beautiful than any other woman—
I am not a poet, Sonya,
I want to live in your hair.

You leapt on my back, I
ran to the shower,
and yes, I slipped on the wet floor—

I watched you gleam in the shower
holding your
breasts in your hand—

two small explosions.

Still Newlyweds

You step out of the shower and the entire nation calms—

a drop of lemon-egg shampoo,
you smell like bees,

a brief kiss,
I don't know anything about you—except the spray of freckles on your shoulders!

which makes me feel so thrillingly

alone.
I stand on earth in my pajamas,

penis sticking out—
for years

in your direction.

Soldiers Aim at Us

They fire
as the crowd of women flees inside the nostrils of searchlights

—may God have a photograph of this—

in the piazza's bright air, soldiers drag Petya's body and his head
bangs the stairs. I

feel through my wife's shirt the shape
of our child.

Soldiers drag Petya up the stairs and homeless dogs, thin as philosophers,
understand everything and bark and bark.

I, now on the bridge, with no camouflage of speech, a body
wrapping the body of my pregnant wife—

Tonight
we don't die and don't die,

the earth is still,
a helicopter eyeballs my wife—

On earth
a man cannot flip a finger at the sky

because each man is already
a finger flipped at the sky.

Army convoy

Hide

Checkpoints

In the streets, soldiers install hearing checkpoints and nail announcements on posts and doors:

> DEAFNESS IS A CONTAGIOUS DISEASE. FOR YOUR OWN PROTECTION ALL SUBJECTS IN CONTAMINATED AREAS MUST SURRENDER TO BE QUARANTINED WITHIN 24 HOURS!

Sonya and Alfonso teach signs in Central Square. When a patrol walks by, they sit on their hands. We see the Sergeant stop a woman on her way to the market, but she cannot hear. He loads her into a truck. He stops another. She does not hear. He loads her into a truck. A third points to her ears.

In these avenues, deafness is our only barricade.

Before the War, We Made a Child

I kissed a woman
whose freckles
arouse the neighbors.

She had a mole on her shoulder
which she displayed
like a medal for bravery.

Her trembling lips
meant *come to bed*.
Her hair waterfalling in the middle

of the conversation meant
come to bed.
I walked in my barbershop of thoughts.

Yes, I thieved her off to bed on the chair
of my hairy arms—
but parted lips

meant *bite my parted lips*.
Lying under the cool
sheets. Sonya!

The things we did.

As Soldiers Choke the Stairwell

As soldiers stomp up the stairs—
my wife's
painted fingernail scratches

and scratches
the skin off her leg, and I feel
the hardness of bone underneath.

It gives me faith.

4 a.m. Bombardment

My body runs in Arlemovsk Street, my clothes in a pillowcase:
I look for a man who looks
exactly like me, to give him my Sonya, my name, my shirt—
It has begun: neighbors climb the trolleys
at the fish market, breaking all
their moments in half. Trolleys burst like intestines in the sun—

Pavel shouts, *I am so fucking beautiful I cannot stand it!*
Two boys still holding tomato sandwiches
hop in the trolley's light, soldiers aim at their faces. Their ears.
I can't find my wife, where is my pregnant wife?
I, a body, adult male, awaits to
explode like a hand grenade.

It has begun: I see the blue canary of my country
pick breadcrumbs from each citizen's eyes—
pick breadcrumbs from my neighbors' hair—
the snow leaves the earth and falls straight up as it should—
to have a country, so important—
to run into walls, into streetlights, into loved ones, as one should—
The blue canary of my country
runs into walls, into streetlights, into loved ones—
The blue canary of my country
watches their legs as they run and fall.

Arrival

You arrive at noon, little daughter, weighing only six pounds. Sonya sets you atop the piano and plays a lullaby no one hears. In the nursery, quiet hisses like a match dropped in water.

Match

Lullaby

Little daughter
rainwater

snow and branches protect you
whitewashed walls

and neighbors' hands all
Child of my Aprils

little earth of
six pounds

my white hair
keeps your sleep lit

Question

What is a child?
A quiet between two bombardments.

While the Child Sleeps, Sonya Undresses

She scrubs me until I spit
soapy water.
Pig, she smiles.

A man should smell better than his country—
such is the silence
of a woman who speaks against silence, knowing

silence moves us to speak.
She throws my shoes
and glasses in the air,

I am of deaf people
and I have
no country but a bathtub and an infant and a marriage bed!

Soaping together
is sacred to us.
Washing each other's shoulders.

You can fuck
anyone—but with whom can you sit
in water?

A Cigarette

Watch—
Vasenka citizens do not know they are evidence of happiness.

In a time of war,
each is a ripped-out document of laughter.

Watch, God—
deaf have something to tell
that not even they can hear.

Climb a roof in Central Square of this bombarded city, you will see—
one neighbor thieves a cigarette,
another gives a dog
a pint of sunlit beer.

You will find me, God,
like a dumb pigeon's beak, I am
pecking
every which way at astonishment.

A Dog Sniffs

Morning.
In a bombed-out street, wind moves the lips of a politician on a poster. Inside, the child Sonya named Anushka suckles. Not sleeping, Alfonso touches his wife's nipple, pulls to his lips a pearl of milk.

Evening.
As Alfonso steps onto Tedna Street in search of bread, the wind brittles his body. Four jeeps pull onto the curb: Sonya is stolen into a jeep as Anushka cries, left behind as the convoy rattles away. The neighbors peek from behind curtains. Silence like a dog sniffs the windowpanes between us.

Curtain

What We Cannot Hear

They shove Sonya into the army jeep
one morning, one morning, one morning in May, one dime-bright morning—

they shove her
and she zigzags and turns and trips in silence

which is a soul's noise.
Sonya, who once said, *On the day of my arrest I will be playing piano.*

We watch four men
shove her—

and we think we see hundreds of old pianos forming a bridge
from Arlemovsk to Tedna Street, and she

waits at each piano—
and what remains of her is

a puppet
that speaks with its fingers,

what remains of a puppet is this woman, what remains
of her (they took you, Sonya)—the voice we cannot hear—is the clearest voice.

Central Square

The arrested are made to walk with their arms raised up. As if they are about to leave the earth and are trying out the wind.

For an apple a peek, soldiers display Sonya, naked, under a TROOPS ARE FIGHTING FOR YOUR FREEDOM poster. Snow swirls in her nostrils. Soldiers circle her eyes with a red pencil. The young soldier aims in the red circle. Spits. Another aims. Spits. The town watches. Around her neck a sign: I RESISTED ARREST.

Sonya looks straight ahead, to where the soldiers are lined up. Suddenly, out of this silence comes her voice, *Ready!* The soldiers raise their rifles on her command.

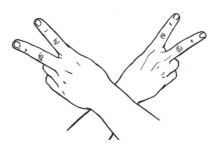

The town watches

A Widower

Alfonso Barabinski stands in Central Square
without a shirt,

rakes up snow and throws it on
marching troops.

His mouth
drives the first syllable of his wife's name into walls—

He, on foot, a good mile and a half of wind,
sets off for the beach, on cobblestone streets, and stops every woman he meets—

Alfonso Barabinski, vodka flask in his pocket, bites a hole in an apple and in that hole
he pours a shot of vodka—

and he drinks *to our health*—
a toast to his wife shot in the center of town where her body

lies down.
Alfonso Barabinski, a child in his arms, spray-paints on the sea wall:
    PEOPLE LIVE HERE—

like an illiterate
signing a document

he does not understand.

For His Wife

I am your boy
drowning in this country, who doesn't know

the word for *drowning*
and yells

I am diving for the last time!

I, This Body

I, this body into which the hand of God plunges,
empty-chested, stand.

At the funeral—
Momma Galya and her puppeteers rise to shake my hand.

I fold our child in a green handkerchief,
brief gift.

You left, my door-slamming wife; and I,
a fool, live.

But the voice I don't hear when I speak to myself is the clearest voice:
when my wife washed my hair, when I kissed

between her toes—
in the empty streets of our district, a bit of wind

called for life.
Wife taken, child

not three days out of the womb, in my arms, our apartment
empty, on the floor

the dirty snow from her boots.

Her Dresses

Her bright dresses
with delicate zippers.

Her ironed
socks.

I stand by
the mirror.

Trying on my wife's red socks.

Elegy

Six words,
Lord:

please ease
of song

my tongue.

Above Blue Tin Roofs, Deafness

Our boys want a public killing in the sunlit piazza.
They drag a drunk soldier, around his neck a sign:
    I ARRESTED THE WOMEN OF VASENKA.
The boys have no idea how to kill a man.
Alfonso signs, *I will kill him for a box of oranges.*
The boys pay a box of oranges.
He cracks a raw egg in a cup,
smells a trickle of oranges in the snow,
and he tosses the egg down his throat like a vodka shot.
He is washing his hands, he is putting on red
socks, he is putting his tongue where his tooth has been.
The girls spit in the soldier's mouth.
A pigeon settles on a stop sign, making it sway.
An idiot boy
whispers, *Long Live Deafness!* and spits at the soldier.
In the center of the piazza
a soldier on his knees begs as townspeople shake their heads, and point at their ears.
Deafness is suspended above blue tin roofs
and copper eaves; deafness
feeds on birches, light posts, hospital roofs, bells;
deafness rests in our men's chests.
Our girls sign, *Start.*
Our boys, wet and freckled, cross themselves.
Tomorrow we will be exposed like the thin ribs of dogs
but tonight
we don't care enough to lie:
Alfonso jumps on the soldier, embraces him, cuts him to the lung.
The soldier flies about the sidewalk.
The town watches the loud animal bones
in their faces and smells the earth.
It is the girls who steal the oranges
and hide them in their shirts.

A City Like a Guillotine Shivers on Its Way to the Neck

Alfonso stumbles from the corpse of the soldier. The townspeople are cheering, elated, pounding him on the back. Those who climbed the trees to watch applaud from the branches. Momma Galya shouts about pigs, pigs clean as men.

At the trial of God, we will ask: why did you allow all this?
And the answer will be an echo: why did you allow all this?

In the Bright Sleeve of the Sky

            Is that you, little soul?
Sometimes at night I

light a lamp so as not
to see.

I tiptoe,
Anushka

drowsing
in my palms:

on my balding head, her bonnet.

To Live

To live is to love, the great book commands.
But love is not enough—

the heart needs a little foolishness!
For our child I fold the newspaper, make a hat

and pretend to Sonya that I am the greatest poet
and she pretends to be alive—

my Sonya, her stories and her eloquent legs,
her legs and stories that open other stories.

(*Stop talking while we are kissing!*)
I see myself—a yellow raincoat,

a sandwich, a piece of tomato between my teeth,
I hoist our infant Anushka to the sky—

(*Old fool*, my wife might have laughed)
I am singing as she pisses

on my forehead and my shoulders!

The Townspeople Watch Them Take Alfonso

Now each of us is
a witness stand:

Vasenka watches us watch four soldiers throw Alfonso Barabinski on the sidewalk.
We let them take him, all of us cowards.

What we don't say
we carry in our suitcases, coat pockets, our nostrils.

Across the street they wash him with firehoses. First he screams,
then he stops.

So much sunlight—
a t-shirt falls off a clothesline and an old man stops, picks it up, presses it to his face.

Neighbors jostle to watch him thrown on the sidewalk like a vaudeville act: *Ta Da*.
In so much sunlight—

each of us
is a witness stand:

They take Alfonso
and no one stands up. Our silence stands up for us.

Away

A soldier marches away from us, carrying Sonya and Alfonso's orphan child. In Central Square, Alfonso hangs from a rope. Urine darkens his trousers.

The puppet of his hand dances.

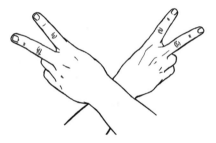

The town watches

Eulogy

You must speak not only of great devastation—

we heard that not from a philosopher
but from our neighbor, Alfonso—

his eyes closed, he climbed other people's porches and recited
to his child our National Anthem:

You must speak not only of great devastation—
when his child cried, he

made her a newspaper hat and squeezed his silence
like two pleats of an accordion:

We must speak not only of great devastation—
and he played that accordion out of tune in a country

where the only musical instrument is the door.

Question

What is a man?
A quiet between two bombardments.

Such Is the Story Made of Stubbornness and a Little Air

Such is the story made of stubbornness and a little air—
a story signed by those who danced wordless before God.
Who whirled and leapt. Giving voice to consonants that rise
with no protection but each other's ears.
We are on our bellies in this quiet, Lord.

Let us wash our faces in the wind and forget the strict shapes of affection.
Let the pregnant woman hold something of clay in her hand.
She believes in God, yes, but also in the mothers
of her country who take off their shoes
and walk. Their footsteps erase our syntax.
Let her man kneel on the roof, clearing his throat
(for the secret of patience is his wife's patience).
He who loves roofs, tonight and tonight, making love to her and to her forgetting,
let them borrow the light from the blind.
There will be evidence, there will be evidence.
While helicopters bomb the streets, whatever they will open, will open.
What is silence? Something of the sky in us.

ACT TWO

The Townspeople Tell the Story of Momma Galya

Story

Townspeople Speak of Galya on Her Green Bicycle

Momma Galya Armolinskaya, 53, is having more sex than any of us.
When she walks across the balcony

a soldier *oh* stands up,
another stands,
then the whole battalion.
We try not to look at her breasts—

they are everywhere,
nipples like bullets.

Wanting to arrest her,
the soldiers
visit her theater—and come back to her theater every night.

By day, Galya aims empty milk bottles at security checkpoints:
on a green bicycle
she flies over the country like
a tardy milkman,
a rim of ice on her bottle caps.

Galya Armolinskaya, the luckiest woman in our nation!
Your iron bicycle tearing with bright
whiskey anthems
through an advancing rank of soldiers into

daylight. You pedal barefoot wearing just
shorts.

And let the law go whistle.

When Momma Galya First Protested

She sucks at a cigarette butt and yells
                              to a soldier,
          Go home! You haven't kissed your wife since Noah was a sailor!

Madame Momma Galya Armolinskaya, what would we give to ride away from our
                              funerals
                    beside you, in a yellow taxi,
          two windows open,
                    leaving loaves of bread
          in the mailboxes
                    of the arrested.

Momma Galya Armolinskaya,
                              by the avenue's wet walls, yells:
          Deafness isn't an illness! It's a sexual position!

A young soldier patrolling a curfew
                    whispers,
          Galya Armolinskaya, yes, Galya Armolinskaya
          whipped a Lieutenant with the leash of his own patrol dog
          and there were thirty-two persons watching
                    (for a baker
                    insisted
          on bringing his sons).

On a night like this God's got an eye on her
                    but she isn't a sparrow.
          In a time of war

          she teaches us how to open the door
                    and walk
                              through
          which is the true curriculum of schools.

A Bundle of Laundry

In Central Square, an army checkpoint. Above the checkpoint, Alfonso's body still hangs from a rope like a puppet of wind. Inside the backroom of the checkpoint, the infant Anushka cries.

In front of the checkpoint, two of Momma Galya's puppeteers climb a park bench and start kissing, hands full of each other's hair. The soldiers are cheering them on and taking bets on how long they will last. The girls smile. *Stop talking while we are kissing!*

Unseen, Momma Galya exits the checkpoint with a bundle of laundry stolen from the Sergeant's clothesline, Anushka hidden in the linens. Snow pours out of the sun.

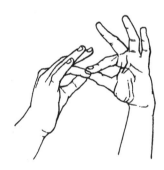

Kiss

What Are Days

Like middle-aged men,
the days of May
walk to prisons.
Like young men they walk to prisons,
overcoats
thrown over their pajamas.

Galya Whispers, as Anushka Nuzzles

In our avenues, election posters show the various hairstyles
of a famous dictator—
and I, at 53
having given up thought of a child, I—(turning to my neighbors and shouting, *Come here!*
Come here!
Marvelous cretins!

She just pooped on the park bench, marvelous cretins!
Parenthood
costs us a little dignity)

—thank God.

Wind sweeps bread from market stalls, shopkeepers spill insults
and the wind already has a bike between its legs—

but when, with a laundry basket out in the streets, I walk,

the wind is helpless
with desire to touch these tiny bonnets and socks.

Galya's Puppeteers

Behind the curtains of the theater, a puppeteer glides her lips over the soldier Ivanoff's penis. He puts one hand on her hair and pulls her to him. She moves the hand away, still kissing him. When his hand is in her hair again, she stops, raises her eyes to him and signs, *Be good*. He takes another swig from his vodka. She takes him in her mouth and closes her eyes. Slides, faster and faster.

Beautiful are the women of Vasenka, beautiful. When she licks the palm of his hand, he laughs. When finally he passes out, she strangles him with a puppet-string. As the soldiers lined up downstairs raise a toast to Momma Galya, they don't see the puppeteers drag the body out back.

Beautiful are the women of Vasenka, beautiful.

Hello, love. The door opens and she motions another soldier to come in.

Be good

In Bombardment, Galya

In the twenty-seventh day of aerial bombardment, I
have nothing except my body, and the walls of this empty apartment flap and flap like a lung.

How to say I only want some quiet; I, a deaf woman, want some quiet, I want some quiet;
I, in the middle of

the nursery where earth asks of me, earth asks of me
too much, I

(before I give up my hiccupping heart and sleep) count
our strength—a woman and a child.

This body I testify from is a binoculars through which you watch, God—
a child clutches a chair,

while the soldiers (their faces are molded from inside by words) arrest all my people, I
run and the flag is the towel the wind dries its hands on.

While they tear off the doors to my empty
apartment—I am in another apartment smiling as the child clutches a chair,

wobbles
toward you and me, God.

I clap and cheer
her first steps,

her first steps, exposed like everybody.

The Little Bundles

While the days of June like middle-aged men
walk to prisons
I cut Anushka's hair:
on her shoulder
on her shoulder
the little bundles pile up.

 •

I am mortal—
I nap.

 •

Anushka, your pajamas—
they are the final meanings of my life.

To get you into your pajamas,
Anushka!

So much to live for.

 •

To bed, Anushka!

I am not deaf
I simply told the world

to shut off its crazy music for a while.

Galya's Toast

To your voice, a mysterious virtue,
to the twenty-six bones of one foot, the four dimensions of breathing,

to pine, redwood, sword fern, peppermint,
to hyacinth and bluebell lily,

to the train conductor's donkey on a rope,
to the smell of lemons, a boy pissing splendidly against the trees.

Bless each thing on earth until it sickens,
until each ungovernable heart admits: *I confused myself*

and yet I loved—and what I loved
I forgot, what I forgot brought glory to my travels,

to you I traveled as close as I dared, Lord.

Theater Nights

On the stage of Galya's theater, a woman bends to cover her coy knees, showing the audience of soldiers the burlesque of her cleavage.

Around her, the stage darkens. The puppeteers drag another strangled soldier into an alleyway.

In the center of the stage Momma Galya strikes a match.

Match

And While Puppeteers Are Arrested

silence?
it is a stick I beat you with, I beat you with a stick, voice, beat you

until you speak, until you
speak right.

Soldiers Don't Like Looking Foolish

Morning. Someone scribbles the names of the arrested and nails the list to the wall. Some names are illegible, just a squiggle, a mustache.

We see Galya's finger tremble down the list.

After detaining every woman on Tedna Street *for what Galya's girls did to soldier Ivanoff*, the army begins to bomb a new store each morning *for what Galya's girls did to soldier Petrovich, for what Galya's girls did to soldier Debenko.*

The streets empty.

A vegetable kiosk explodes, a tomato flies toward us and falls apart in the wind.

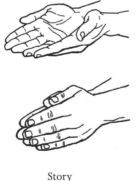

Story

Search Patrols

I cover the eyes of Gena, 7, and Yasha, 9,
as their father drops his trousers to be searched, and his flesh shakes

and around him:
silence's gross belly flaps. The crowd watches.

The children watch us watch:
soldiers drag a naked man up the staircase. I teach his children's hands to make of anguish

a language—
see how deafness nails us into our bodies. Anushka

speaks to homeless dogs as if they are men,
speaks to men

as if they are men
and not just souls on crutches of bone.

Townspeople
watch children but feel under the bare feet of their thoughts

the cold stone of the city.

Lullaby

I look at you, Anushka,
and say

to the late
caterpillars

goodmorning, Senators!
This is a battle

worthy
of our weapons!

Firing Squad

On balconies, sunlight. On poplars, sunlight, on our lips.
Today no one is shooting.
A girl cuts her hair with imaginary scissors—
the scissors in sunlight, her hair in sunlight.
Another girl nicks a pair of shoes from a sleeping soldier, skewered with light.
As soldiers wake and gape at us gaping at them,
what do they see?
Tonight they shot fifty women on Lerna Street.
I sit down to write and tell you what I know:
a child learns the world by putting it in her mouth,
a girl becomes a woman and a woman, earth.
Body, they blame you for all things and they
seek in the body what does not live in the body.

Question

What is a woman?
A quiet between two bombardments.

Yet, I Am

Yet, I am. I exists. I has
a body.
When Anushka

takes my finger
in her mouth, she
bites.

How do we live on earth, child?
If I could hear
you, what would you say?

Your answer!

On earth we can do
—can't we?—

what we want.

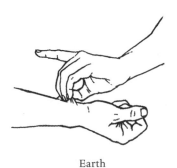

Earth

The Trial

Wearing a child like a broken arm, Galya sidles through Central Square. Of the buildings bombed on Tedna Street, only door frames are left standing. Doors and puppets dangling from their handles, a puppet for every shot citizen.

From the sidewalks, neighbors watch two women step in front of Galya. *My sister was arrested because of your revolution,* one spits in her face. Another takes her by the hair, *I will open your skull and scramble your eggs!* They grab Anushka, then drag Galya behind the bakery.

The market fills with shopkeepers yawning and unpacking their wares. The stallkeepers sweep. Galya stumbles out from the alley, clutching first one neighbor, then another. She runs after the woman holding Anushka. They push her away with their brooms.

She shouts.

They point to their ears.

Gracefully, our people shut their windows.

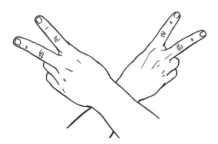

The crowd watches

Pursued by the Men of Vasenka

We see her zigzag between us in the street—
her face slashed

like a zipper stuck in her coat—
My dear neighbors! she yells,

My dear neighbors! Marvelous cretins!
She yells at us like that.

Dig a good hole!
Lay me nostrils up

and shovel in my mouth the decent black earth.

Anonymous

And as for Momma Galya's coffin, it got chocked
in the stairwell and we had to carry it upside down.

There were too many bodies and
not enough people—
too many ears and no one attached to them.

In this time
each person does something for our country.
Some die.
Others give speeches.

Too many people and not enough hands
to wash Momma Galya's body and trim her fingernails—
the last
courtesy
shown in our land.

Today
I have to screw on the expression of a person

though I am at most an animal
and the animal I am spirals

from the funeral to his kitchen, shouts: *I have come, God, I have come running to you—*
in snow-drifted streets, I stand like a flagpole

without a flag.

And Yet, on Some Nights

Our country has surrendered.

Years later, some will say none of this happened; the shops were open, we were happy and went to see puppet shows in the park.

And yet, on some nights, townspeople dim the lights and teach their children to sign. Our country is the stage: when patrols march, we sit on our hands. *Don't be afraid*, a child signs to a tree, a door.

When patrols march, the avenues empty. Air empties, but for the squeaks of strings and the *tap tap* of wooden fists against the walls.

We are sitting in the audience, still. Silence, like the bullet that's missed us, spins—

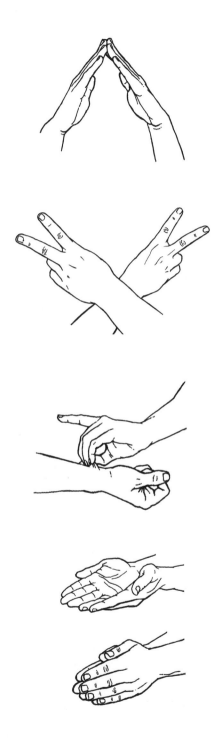

In a Time of Peace

Inhabitant of earth for fortysomething years
I once found myself in a peaceful country. I watch neighbors open

their phones to watch
a cop demanding a man's driver's license. When the man reaches for his wallet, the cop
shoots. Into the car window. Shoots.

It is a peaceful country.

We pocket our phones and go.
To the dentist,
to pick up the kids from school,
to buy shampoo
and basil.

Ours is a country in which a boy shot by police lies on the pavement
for hours.

We see in his open mouth
the nakedness
of the whole nation.

We watch. Watch
others watch.

The body of a boy lies on the pavement exactly like the body of a boy—

It is a peaceful country.

And it clips our citizens' bodies
effortlessly, the way the President's wife trims her toenails.

All of us
still have to do the hard work of dentist appointments,
of remembering to make
a summer salad: basil, tomatoes, it is a joy, tomatoes, add a little salt.

This is a time of peace.

I do not hear gunshots,
but watch birds splash over the backyards of the suburbs. How bright is the sky
as the avenue spins on its axis.
How bright is the sky (forgive me) how bright.

Notes

ON SIGNS: In Vasenka, the townspeople invented their own sign language. Some of the signs derived from various traditions (Russian, Ukrainian, Belarusian, American Sign Language, etc.). Other signs might have been made up by citizens, as they tried to create a language not known to authorities.

ON SILENCE: The deaf don't believe in silence. Silence is the invention of the hearing.

Acknowledgments

"We Lived Happily during the War" is for Eleanor Wilner.
"Gunshot" is for Jericho Brown.
"Deafness, an Insurgency, Begins" is for Boris and Ludmila Khersonsky.
"That Map of Bone and Opened Valves" is for Brian Turner.
"Four a.m. Bombardment" is for Denis Johnson.
"A Cigarette" is for Sherhiy Zhadan.
"Firing Squad" is for Garth Greenwell.
"In a Time of Peace" is for Carolyn Forché and Patricia Smith.

All love poems are for Katie Farris.

/ / /

I am grateful to the editors of the following journals, where some of these poems have appeared, often in different forms: *Alaska Quarterly Review*, *The American Poetry Review*, *The Café Review*, *Columbia: A Journal of Literature and Art*, *Cork Literary Review*, *Gulf Coast*, *Harvard Review*, *Image*, *The Kenyon Review*, *Lana Turner*, *The Massachusetts Review*, *McSweeney's*, *The New Yorker*, *Ploughshares*, *Poetry*, *Poetry Review* (UK), *Poetry Wales*, *A Public Space*, *Runes*, *Seneca Review*, *The Shop* (Ireland), *Spillway*, *Wolf*, and *World Literature Today*.

I am also grateful to the editors of the following anthologies where some of these poems have appeared: *The Best American Poetry* (Scribner, 2018), *American Journal: Fifty Poems for Our Time* (Graywolf, 2018), *Resistance, Rebellion, Life: 50 Poems Now* (Knopf, 2017), *Poems for Political Disaster* (Boston Review, 2017), *The Mighty Stream: Poems in Celebration of Martin Luther King* (Bloodaxe Books, 2017), *Liberation: New Works on Freedom from Internationally Renowned Poets* (Beacon Press, 2015), *The Wolf Anthology* (Wolf, 2012), *Sunken Garden Poetry: 1992–2011* (Wesleyan University

Press, 2012), *Pushcart Prize Anthology* (Pushcart Press, 2012), *I Go to the Ruined Place: Contemporary Poems in Defense of Global Human Rights* (Lost Horse Press, 2010), *New Poets of the American West* (Many Voices Press, 2010), *Between Water and Song: New Poets for the Twenty-First Century* (White Pine Press, 2010), *13 Younger Contemporary American Poets* (Proem Press, 2009), *From the Fishhouse: An Anthology of Poems That Sing, Rhyme, Resound, Syncopate, Alliterate, and Just Plain Sound Great* (Persea Books, 2009), and the Poem-a-Day Series of the Academy of American Poets.

I am grateful to the following people for helping me to become a better person and writer: Kaveh Akbar, Sandra Alcosser, Hari Alluri, Catherine Barnett, Polina Barskova, Calvin Bedient, Sherwin Bitsui, Malachi Black, Jericho Brown, James Byrne, Ali Calderon, Victoria Chang, Adam Davis, Kwame Dawes, Chard DeNiord, Ming Di, Blas Falconer, Carolyn Forché, Katie Ford, Jeff Friedman, Carol Frost, Rachel Galvin, Forrest Gander, David Gewanter, Garth Greenwell, Edward Hirsch, Jane Hirshfield, Matthew Hollis, J. Hope Stein, Lizz Huerta, Ishion Hutchinson, Susan Kelly DeWitt, David Keplinger, Kerry Keys, Suji Kwock Kim, Steve Kowitt, Li-Young Lee, Dana Levin, Jeffrey Levine, James Longenbach, Thomas Lux, Ruth Madievsky, Nikola Madzirov, Dora Malech, David Tomas Martinez, David Matlin, Philip Metres, Malena Mörling, Valzhyna Mort, Mihaela Moscaliuc, Sandeep Parmar, Charles Pratt, Mary Rakow, Tomaz Salamun, Jim Schley, Don Share, Charles Simic, Peter Streckfus, Sam Taylor, Susan Terris, Katherine Towler, Brian Turner, Jean Valentine, Alissa Vales, Adam Veal, G. C. Waldrep, Michael Waters, Karry Wayson, Eleanor Wilner, Christian Wiman, Adam Zagajewski, and Matthew Zapruder.

Thanks also to Jennifer Whitten and Gail Schneider for the gift of their artwork.

Thanks to the Guggenheim Foundation, Lannan Foundation, Poetry Foundation, Whiting Foundation, MacDowell, Virginia Center for Creative Arts, Vermont Studio Center, Faber and Faber, and Tupelo Press for their support.

/ / /

Deepest gratitude to Graywolf Press and especially to Jeff Shotts for his faith in this book.

ILYA KAMINSKY was born in the former Soviet Union and is now an American citizen. He is the author of *Dancing in Odessa*, and coeditor of *The Ecco Anthology of International Poetry*. He was a 2014 finalist for the Neustadt International Prize for Literature. His other honors include a Guggenheim Fellowship, a Lannan Literary Fellowship, and a Whiting Award. His work has been translated into more than twenty languages.

The text of *Deaf Republic* is set in Dante MT Pro.

Book design by Rachel Holscher.

Composition by Bookmobile Design and Digital Publisher Services,
    Minneapolis, Minnesota.

Manufactured by Versa Press on acid-free, 30 percent postconsumer wastepaper.